Coming Through The Storm

Author: Melinda Limbeck-Currie

First Printing

Publication of: Irish Writing Service

Imprint: Trenton Stories

ISBN: 978-0692547779

Printed in the United States of America

C O N T E N T S

DEDICATIONS

To my oldest daughter Tanji Glenne' Jones better known to me by your nickname (T) and my unborn grandchild. Thanks for the day that you said, "We got our mother's back." Those words meant a lot to me years ago and they still mean the world to me.

To Candice Marie, and Brandice Leigh, better known to me by your nicknames, (Can-Can & Bam-Bam) God knew what he was doing when he gave me two. The love bond you have with each other is priceless, and I hope you never lose it.

To my one and only grandchild, Trenton Thomas Jones, you change the game for my life. Thanks for rescuing me all over again. Your G-ma loves you forever.

Every time my heart beats, it beats for all four of you. I love you all very much, thanks for loving me unconditionally, and believing in me through all the good, bad ugly. My life is complete and I'm grateful to God that I have each one of you at arms reach.

ACKNOWLEDEGMENT

First I would like to thank Jesus Christ for saving, loving and healing me. Thanks for keeping your hand on my life all my life. Thanks Holy Spirit for giving me the strength and ability to write my book.

My Father John Limbeck Sr., and my mother Helen Yvonne Limbeck who has passed from this life to the next. I'm truly my father's daughter because I resemble him in so many ways. In all the fast life he lived, I thank God that I was able to see the many good things that he did for others. He was a man with a heart of gold. My mother was the foundation of my life, through her relationship with God and the life she lived through Him. She showed me how to be a Christian, way before I accepted God into my life. Rest easy dear mother for God always had a plan and now I'm walking in it.

Granddad & grandma Jay & Rose Limbeck, with all that we went through I always felt your love for me and I thank God for that.

Mark and Dave Limbeck, my biological brothers; who has gone from this life to the next. I love you both and miss you more than words can say. Even though it was many years ago, I shall never forget the times that my brother Mark showed me how to play sports, it holds dear to my heart. I will never forget all the fun, and cook-outs we had at Dave's house, those memories will be with me forever.

My brother's Johnny Jr., George, Daniel aka (Boone), Stephen aka (Stevie), and Scotty, I love you all very much, and I'm glad I still have each of you in my life. Johnny I want to thank you for all your advice and encouragement over the years, it means so much to me.

Eric Jones, you are not only a good husband to my daughter and a wonderful father to my grandson, but you are also a blessing to have as a son-in-law.

My Pastor, Frank Glenn Jr. and the Glenn Christian Church; my life would be empty without this ministry. God used you and this house of worship to bring me to a place of healing and total deliverance.

Pastor Kent Barnes of One Nation Kingdom Ministries; thanks for your words of encouragement. You always said for me, "To know my potential." Thanks for your kindness toward me and my children. I can now see why you and my brother Mark were such good friends.

Carolyn Little, my BFF; thank you for loving me unconditionally even when I didn't know how to be a friend, you always stayed true. Thirty years of friendship and going strong, I love you.

Karen Lewis aka (momma Karen), now your word has come to pass, years ago you said "Girl you better write your book." Thanks for your encouragement.

Shawn Currie; thanks for loving me to this very day and staying my friend. Felicia Bullett my sister you're an inspiration to me, friend and prayer partner thanks for all your support.

Welton Glenn Thomas, aka (Doc) in the words of a good man, "Keep your heart in God's hands."

Mrs. Dorothy Thomas (my children's grandmother) whom has passed from this life to the next; I will never forget how you cared for my children, rest in peace.

Henrietta Rable, having you around is like having my mother back in my life. Thanks for being in our lives.

Sarah Edmonds, thanks for all the fun events that we always attend, especially the hot and spicy at the Chinese restaurant.

Shari Boffman, in the past we had a lot of good times, I love you.

Danova Barnes and your daughter DaNazja thanks for your hospitality while allowing me to spend many hours in your home while writing my book. I love ya'll.

Farrah Jones it's a joy when I see you, and I always enjoy our talks on the porch. I'll always remember your precious baby Na'Kyiah she was the loving angel that God allowed us to have for a season.

Andre Jones aka (Dre) I will always remember the good times we had, and I will always be your friend.

Irish Jordan, I'm so happy to see how God uses you in your writing gift. The day I saw you in church and said "I would like to write a book." You said, "I can show you how." That day has changed my life. Thanks for the long hours together and being my friend, because this is bigger than a book. I love you.

Wayne and Renee Truss, thanks for believing in me, Renee you said I need to write my book. Now it has come to pass, I appreciate your words of encouragement.

Lizette Star-Currie for all the times you made me laugh you are truly missed.

Mrs. Myrtle Currie aka (Nam) you were an inspiration to us all and we are grateful for all your prayers. You lived ninety blessed years of love.

I'm sending out a shout to my friend Marvin Brown God bless you.

My two toy poodles; Sugar and Chloe', thanks for loving me back. Usually people rescue animals but this time two wonderful dogs rescued me.

Chapter 1

Growing Up

As a little girl my mother always took me to church. My mother loved God and lived a life of true relationship unto Him. I can remember how we would sit on the porch of our house and she would read bible stories to me.

I was born in Ohio in a family of eight children, with brothers that were great athletes. My oldest brother (Johnny Limbeck) broke track records, in our local west-side high school and my fourth oldest brother (Mark Limbeck) now deceased, was MVP with our local west-side high school football team. The athletic ability was in the blood, and coming from a house with athletic brothers I learned to play many different sports and I was really good at playing soft ball.

As I grew a little older my mother told me, I was born with cancer. She said the doctor told her that this was a rare form of cancer and I wouldn't live pass six months old. This type of cancer made my bottom lip have a permanent purple color and I had a large growth growing on the left side of my head.

My grandmother (my mother's mother) told my mother to take me to a particular faith healing ministry that she believed in, that was located in Youngstown, Ohio. My grandmother and my mother's brother drove me to this ministry.

Once we arrived at this ministry, we took a seat in the balcony. The pastor would always call people out and name the conditions or aliments that were present in a person's life.

This particular day, she pointed up to the balcony where my mother was holding me and the pastor said "A baby is being healed right now of cancer." Even though I didn't know at that time but now I can say that baby was me.

A week later my mother took me back for my check-up, the doctor with excitement on his face said "It's gone, it's gone!" He was referring to the cancer that was previously in my body. My mother ask the doctor, "Do you believe in the power of prayer?" He answered, "I do now." This was my first miracle. It's amazing how the plan of the devil was trying to stop my life at the birth gate, but God had the ultimate plan!

On my mother's side of the family it was God fearing, influential people, preachers and teachers of the gospel.

By the time I was a teenager my mother was sick and in the hospital a lot. At this point my younger brother's were living at home with my father. My father was a heavy drinker and had affairs with multiple women while married to my mother. He was a very hard working man for a local steel mill; however he didn't always bring home the money to help take care of his eight children.

My father's parents owned a bar called Jay's lounge on the west side of town. After the closing hours of Jay's lounge, my grandmother would sell drinks and allow people to play cards.

Even though I was a teenager, my father's mother would take me and my two brothers to Jay's lounge to help her clean up sometimes. Other times we would sit at one of the tables and do our homework, and if no customers were around me and my brothers were allowed to shoot pool.

I can remember there were many days that the lounge was very crowded with people drinking, smoking, and playing pool.

One day at Jay's lounge I was twelve years old, me and my younger brother's were outside in the parking lot playing catch and there was an older man that would always look at me in a way that made me feel uncomfortable.

This day he came outside behind me and my brother's. He walked over to me and whispered, "You look so pretty, I can buy you some chips and pop." I knew it was not right even as a young child, I never told nobody about this man, but I thank God he never touched me because I knew he wanted to.

At age fourteen I accepted the Lord Jesus Christ into my life. I can remember it like yesterday; I got on my knees in front of a chair and ask the Lord Jesus to come into my heart. At age fifteen I was standing in my parents bedroom praying and I spoke in tongues.

A couple years later I was out one night with a girl friend and there was a band playing. At intermission a guy from the band walked up to the bar where I was sitting. I turned and asked him "Would you play a song by Marvin Gaye?" He answered "Only if you let me get your telephone number." I gave him my telephone number and we became an item.

That year I made the cheerleading team in high school and I later found out I was pregnant with our first child (Tanji). I gave up my cheerleading spot to one of my classmates that wanted to be on the team with her sister.

Being the only girl I lived with my grandmother (father's mother) in her two story home located right across the street from my parent's house. My grandmother rented rooms from her two story home to people that were in need of a place to live.

Chapter 2

Don't Wear Black

My grandmother (father's mother) had a house on the west-side and she had several very pretty women prostitutes that were of different nationalities living there. My grandmother was the madam and always carried her pistol.

On my father's side of the family I grew up around prostitutes, gamblers, fast money and a line of hustler's.

My grandmother had the women set up with all their needs met such as food, clothes, and living arrangements. The johns would come and go; my grandmother would come by on the weekend to pick up the money from the women. There was no pimps on this scene, my grandmother would give the women their half and make sure everything was in order at the house.

My grandfather worked at a local steel mill but not the one that my father worked for. One late night at Jay's lounge my grandfather was behind the bar, the door buzzer went off and he let a young lady in who said she wanted a squirt soda.

When she bought her soda she left the door propped open, and one guy came in with a sawed off shot gun, to rob my grandfather, but my grandfather refused to give up the money. The robber shot him, and in fear the gunman ran; never taking the money from the cash register. My grandfather was shot, but somehow he still made it to the telephone and called the house. I answered the telephone, his last words were, "Tell your grandma I been shot." He died on the way to the hospital.

Later the gunman's brother who was the driver came back to the scene acting as if he never knew what happened. However a guy from across the street was looking out his window during the entire robbery and informed the police of the identities of the robbers.

The shooter and the driver went to prison for a long stretch and the lady that propped the door turned evidence and took a plea deal, and was not given any time.

After the death of my grandfather, the man that my grandmother was married to for forty years was now gone from her life, and she was never the same. Her mind was slowly leaving and she got really sick as her health went down hill.

At this point my father took over Jay's lounge, and sold the house where the prostitutes were staying.

Now I'm about nineteen years old and I became one of the bar maids for a couple years.

About eight years later while still living with my grandmother I got pregnant again. My parents and my grandparents did try to help me at first. As time went on my parents were not getting any younger, they had raised eight children and helped me with my first child (Tanji). I could tell they were not up for the challenge of raising another child.

After a while I moved out of my grandmother's house and in with the children's father on the west-side of the city. At that point we found out I was pregnant with twins.

My pregnancy with the twins was very hard, I developed toxemia. I carried them full term, they were nine pounds each. I believe at that time they were the largest twins born in our city.

After delivery of the twins I went into a coma for a day, when I regained consciousness my brother Mark helped us name our twins. I was very thin, I had lost so much weight, and my blood pressure was out of control. The doctor wanted to send the twins home and keep me longer. I was not going to allow that to happen, so they permitted me to go home with my babies.

My mother would come over from time to time and give me a helping hand. After many days God healed my body and I was able to fully take care of my twins.

Six months later my children's father and I took a night out to ourselves while my grandmother watched all three of the children over at her house. That morning I was awakened by a telephone call from my mother telling me that my oldest daughter (eight years old) called her and said, "Grandma is dead."

Once the ambulance got there they said my grandmother had a massive heart attack while sitting in the chair at the kitchen table. My twins (six months) were still sleeping in the back room through the entire incident.

My grandmother always told me when she dies that I'm not to wear the color black to her funeral. I honored her request and wore a pink skirt, and a bright colored blouse with a bright red London fog coat.

She left me her roomy fenced-in home and nice car. Me the children and baby daddy immediately moved out of the house we were in and into my grandmother's house.

Over the years Jay's lounge was never the same; there was a lot of fighting, and shootings in the parking lot. My father was no longer happy with the lounge. From time to time there would be good moments like the champion boxer would come and hang out at Jay's lounge, someone would loudly announce "The champ is here!"

We would set out drinks, and everyone in the lounge would have a good time. During that time I went out a couple times with one of the boxing champions. He was older, and treated me with much respect like a lady is supposed to be treated, and we had big fun together.

Years later we sold the bar, and my father said we literally gave it away for the price that it was sold at. I remember my father saying "This lounge has become more of a curse than anything else, and it was time to give it up."

Not long after that my father got saved accepting Jesus Christ into his life.

I felt so sad living in my grandmother's house without her being there; everything reminded me of her, and I missed her a lot. I had to accept the reality that this was now my house.

Chapter 3

In The Dark

About one year after moving into my grandmother's house I felt I needed to talk to a professional and I started visiting a counseling service in my city. One day during one of my counseling sessions my psychiatrist prescribed me a prescription by the name of Quaalude. After taking them over a period of time I found myself self medicating with other prescriptions such as valiums.

Couple months later after the prescription drugs no longer took the effect that they once had, I got introduced to cocaine and it was off and running.

First it started out as a little fun then like all street drugs; it may start out as fun, but then the drugs do you. Before I knew it I was completely hooked, like what you would call a full blown junky. I started lying stealing and doing anything I could to get high.

It was now to a point in my life because of my addiction, I allowed people to use my house to sell, and cook up their drugs. We would be in the house lighting up the cocaine pipe for days at a time. My girls would be watching television in the back room and I would give instructions to my oldest to keep an eye on the twins.

At one time I got a sack of my own to sell, but it didn't work because I would use too much of my own product. I learned that it's hard to sell and use at the same time, one will win out the other.

I can remember on a particular day I smoked so much that I smoked myself sober, I mean I literally smoked myself sober.

On a particular occasion I was home by myself, a guy came by and knocked on the door I was familiar with his face so I let him in and he walked to the back room as normal. When he closed the door he pulled a gun out and said, "Give me all the money you got on you right now."

I looked at him with an expression of surprise, but in fear I gave him all the money that I had on me. After he left I thought to myself, "I've just been robbed."

By this time me and the children's father were not on the greatest terms, the drugs had us arguing all the time about one thing or another. It got so bad I change the lock on my doors and put him out.

I started seeing a high-roller from Detroit that I really liked, and he liked me a lot too. He would buy my children's clothes, and bring groceries to the house. He would never put money in my hand because he knew I would go get some drugs.

He would try and tell me to stop using and he refuse to give me any drugs. (You know it's bad when a drug dealer won't sell to you). Finally he decided this area of Ohio was no longer working for him and he moved back to Detroit.

In the summer of that year, my lights got shut off, and someone turned them back on for me but it was done illegally. That worked for a while, until the bill got to be about a thousand dollars and they got shut off again and this time they stayed off a long time.

My oldest daughter went to live across the street with my parents and my twins went to live with their father's mother. After that the water went off, I would go across the street to my parent's house and take baths, eat and fill my milk jugs with water and take them back across the street to my house.

I'm so grateful to God that I never lost my children to the system. They were still able to see each other a lot and were close sisters. Nobody but God allowed them to be well taken care of during my addiction. I never forgot the words that my mother said to me one day, "Melinda if you miss your children growing up, you miss everything."

Now here I am in this big house that my grandmother has left me with no water, no lights and no food. I was feeling so empty, because crack cocaine leaves you feeling that way. Yet, I was still sitting in this dark empty house using candles to smoke cocaine, and a flash light at night to see around the house.

At this time my father had come up with a rule for their home that me and my brother had to follow. He said "No more coming in my house any hours of the night, if you want to come to this house you must be in here by twelve midnight". Now at this point remember, my lights, water and gas is turned off, and people around the neighborhood know it.

One night I didn't want to go to my house so I decided to do what I usually do and go to my parent's house across the street. I knocked on the door and my father came to the window and he asked, "What do you want it's after midnight?" I looked up to the window and said, "Open the door daddy it's raining out here." He said, "Didn't I tell you and your brother that if you want to get in this house you better be in here by midnight?" Still looking up to the window at my father as the rain is coming down on my face I said, "It's raining and cold daddy open the door." My father just closed the window and pulled the curtain over the window.

I just stood there for a minute, and then started walking back across the street toward my house; just then the neighbor stuck his head out his door. He said, "Hey, what's wrong?" I said, "My father won't let me in, he's using that old crazy rule." The neighbor said, "You don't have to go over to that dark house, you can come over here."

I walked into their house and he said, "You can sit at the kitchen table and keep warm until day break, cause if you wake up my father we both will be out in the cold and rain." I sat at the neighbor's table all night doing the head bob trying to keep from falling asleep. As soon as daybreak came I left and went next door to my parents.

I decided it was time for me to go and get some help. I knew I needed a really intense program but because I couldn't afford one I went to the local hospital, and was admitted on the psychiatric floor.

I stayed there for about ten days as they gave me all types of medication. Inside I felt beat down, like I would never conqueror this addiction. I remember in my spirit I heard the words, "I'll beat it for you."

I was released from the hospital and back at home. I can remember trying to stay clean, but as the same people would come and knock on my door, it brought back old memories. Before long I was at it again smoking cocaine for about ninety days.

I went back into the hospital but this time, I knew I needed something more than last time.

They sent someone in from a really strong program. The counselor came and had a consultation with me that went very well. I told him "I don't need to be on this floor with these crazy people, I need a more intense drug addiction program." He came back the next day and said, "We have one bed available, but there's three people that are eligible for it."

After all was said and done the final decision was made to allow me to have the charity bed for the twenty-eight day program. It was a great program and I met a lot of people. They gave me plenty of tools on how to stay clean and sober. I gained weight I got healthy while working the program.

After all that it wasn't even thirty days and I was back at it full force. That whole people, places and things, had won. Within the next sixty days I was spending all the bill monies on drugs and sitting in my house with no lights and smoking dope with candles.

It's summer time, I tried selling the drugs again and I had one of my male friends cook up the cocaine at his house on the west-side, because remember I can't cook at home no gas, water or lights.

One weekend my male friend that does the cooking for me left me and my girl friend at his house with my product.

Two guys pulled in the driveway and said, "Let me get a twenty bag." Next thing I know they rushed in through the back door and shot at the girl that was there with me.

I wasn't for sure if she was hit, I ran into the living room and screamed out, "Don't shoot me in the name of Jesus!" One of the guys said, "Stop saying that." It didn't matter to me what he said I continued to scream it over and over. Isn't it funny that even in all the mess I was in I still would call on the name of Jesus.

They took all the monies and the drugs and ran out to their car. Once they were gone I went over to check on my girlfriend, she was passed out from the fear and the bullet was in the wood of the floor next to her. That was the last time I tried to sell drugs.

Chapter 4

Catch Me If You Can

Now I'm walking the street all hours of the night being with men I didn't care anything about, it was all about feeding my addiction.

One night in the car with a male, as we were getting high on crack he decided he wanted to act real crazy while we're parked behind a building. He grabbed my arm and tried to put a handcuff on my wrist and cuff me to his steering wheel.

I was fighting him with my free hand and lifted my leg up and kicked him. I released the door and jumped out running, and then he jumped out and chased me.

While I was running I looked back and he was still coming behind me with an angry look on his face. I picked up speed and out ran him. Once I was out of his site I slowed down, as I was breathing hard I said to myself, "You can't catch no Limbeck."

Another night I'm back at my house, with a male friend; my house is now a complete dope house. After smoking crack for a couple hours; he looked at me and said, "You better give me back my dope." I ask, "What you talking about?" He said, "You know you stole some of my dope off this table." I said, "Ain't nobody take nothing from you, now here you go talking about I done stole something from you." Then he took out his straight razor; and said in a loud tone, "You better give me my stuff." And again I said, "Didn't nobody take nothing from you." He raised his hand with the straight razor and sliced me across the side of my face.

Just then someone knocked on my door, when I opened my door he quickly walked out. Of course I never called the police because what would I say, "I took his dope."

About a week later, I was out at a club and decided to go home with a guy. Once in the bedroom he shut the door. I noticed there were extension cords every where, but once we start getting high on crack I didn't think anything about the cords. After a while he was really gee-ked and he stood up and pushed the dresser in front of the closed bedroom door. Because the dresser was heavier than he could handle, he couldn't make it fit all the way across the door.

He got the extension cords and tried to tie me up, and I began fighting him for my life. I broke away from him and got through the open section of the dresser that was in front of the bedroom door. I ran out of there as fast as I could and didn't look back.

A night out in Youngstown, Ohio a couple of my usual girlfriends and I were hanging out, and I noticed one of them left with a truck driver and I didn't see her anymore that night.

The next night I went back and still didn't see her, I asked around but none of the girls had seen her since last night either. A couple days later I read the newspaper and her picture was in the paper.

She had been found dead and raped left in a ditch. To this day I always thought it was that truck driver serial rapist that was going around killing women and he passed through Youngstown, Ohio.

Months later another one of the girls that I hung out with was found dead in a hotel, they said the cause of death was an over dose of heroine.

Chapter 5

They Was Waiting On Me

At home feeling down and a little depressed, I decided to go over a friend's house. Once I got in the door and sat down, I could tell something was going on in the back room, so I made my way back there.

They had some crack and drink laid out, I joined in and after a while I didn't want anymore and decided I was going home.

When I walked outside it was dark, there was a nice car pulling in the driveway. The driver asked me, "Do you need a ride?" I looked at him and said to myself, "He look good." I answered, "I'm not sure." He asked, "What's your name?" I answered "Melinda Limbeck." He said in excitement, "Oh wow, I went to school with your brother Johnny, my name is Sean."

That made me feel comfortable and I got in the car and let him drive me home. Before I got out of the car he ask me for my telephone number and I gave it to him.

The next day, he called me and we went out together. Before long we were an item and I moved in with him. My children were still staying with their grandparents, so it was just me and Sean in his apartment.

Not long after I moved in with Sean one of his family members got me a job at a doctor's office on the other side of town. It was like putting a kid in a candy store. I started out with the responsibility of filing the charts in alphabetical order and then they moved me to work as the doctor's office assistant.

He was a brilliant man, and even paid into a couple scholarships to send less fortunate children to school. It wasn't long till I began to take the office sample pain pills to self medicate myself. When we were out of office samples I even wrote prescriptions in fictitious names to get the pain pills. This job really made things worst for my addiction.

Sean decided we should get married and he ask me, I said no. It was like there was no way around it because his family and my family were church goers and were telling us that we should be married and not continue to live in a sinful situation.

Months later he ask me again, I said, "Yes, but I want a church wedding."

On the day of my wedding everybody was waiting for me to walk down the aisle. I was in the bathroom fixing my hair, putting lipstick on and getting high. Once I could get out the bathroom, we had a small but beautiful wedding. My mother gave me away due to my father was bed ridden with an illness and could not come to my wedding.

For the reception everyone went back to my parent's house to celebrate, so we could spend some time with my father in his time of illness. I felt very happy with my husband and both our families together.

My children didn't come live with us they continued being taken care of by their grandparents.

Back to work, still writing prescriptions to self medicate myself. It got really bad and I knew I had to make a change. My husband had really good insurance so I went into a very expensive rehabilitation center this time.

I was granted a thirty day stay, but fourteen days in I got really sick. They had to transport me out of the rehabilitation center to a hospital in Pennsylvania. I was hearing voices and couldn't eat, the opioids had me crazy. They put me on the psych ward, it was terrible. The doctors gave me some medicine and I did feel better and eventually was back feeling normal.

On one of my husband's visits to see me, I told him to sneak me in some dope. He just looked at me and he shook his head in disbelief. He never did sneak me any in and I finished out my thirty day stay in that hospital and was released home.

When I got home I sat my luggage down and went straight to the dope man's house. I never went back to work at the doctor's office. Over time I lost weight, and again was feeling empty; it seemed like I just couldn't beat this drug addiction.

Over the next few weeks I was still getting high, but I would push and make myself go to church. While in church my pastor would come out into the aisle and ask did anyone need prayer.

I would walk out into the aisle and say, "Yes, I need prayer to be delivered from drugs." They would lay hands on me and pray.

After some years of marriage me and Sean seem to grow apart. The drugs and alcohol played a big part in our relationship and we decided to divorce.

Chapter 6

Traveling

I wanted a change in location so I traveled to Vegas with a male friend for a weekend stay. We ended up staying for a couple months; I worked at the Gentlemen's Club where the men were not allowed to touch the women.

One night a man followed me to my car after work. As I got in my car he put his hands on my shoulder and he tried to pull me out of my car. I started screaming, "Let me go let me go!" Another guy came up that I'd never seen before and said, "Man let her go." He let me go and he walked away, the other guy asks me, "Are you alright?" I answered, "Yea, I'll be fine." I put my key in the ignition and drove back to the hotel room.

Later that week my male friend told me we needed to make a drive to Mexico. Once we arrived we got a hotel and stayed for about a week. While in Mexico, we went out to a bar; my male friend got us a table and after I was seated he walked over to a couple guys that were from Mexico and they started talking. I could see from their hand motions and body language that something was not right, it looked like they were arguing.

When he came back to the table he looked at me and said, "We got to get packed and get out of Mexico tonight." At that point I was so afraid; I felt we were running for our lives. I thought to myself; "What is going on, do he owe these people money?" Whatever the deal was we got back to the hotel and packed up and left Mexico immediately.

By the time we made it back to Vegas, my money was low. I went back to the gentlemen's club and stacked my money so I could get back to Ohio. While at the gentlemen's club I asked about one of the regular dancers, and I was told she was found in the desert dead a couple days before I got back.

After I made enough money, my male friend and I drove back to Ohio. I moved in with my parents, but I still had my house (which was a dope house) across the street

Chapter 7

Left For Dead

I went to a local bar on the west-side of town. I found someone to sell me some crack, I gave him the money and when I opened the package it wasn't crack cocaine. I got upset that he had beat me for my money.

Within the next hour I seen him walking in the bar parking lot and I said in my mind, "There he go." I turned on the car and hit the gas paddle; as the car was moving very fast toward him right before hitting him the car engine just cut off; I mean it literally cut off. He turned and looked at me with anger knowing I was trying to run him down.

He came to my side of the car and yelled for his boys to come over to the car. He hit me in the head with a forty ounce beer bottle. They threw at least five forty-ounce bottles at my head that cut my head wide open at the hair line and over my eye brow.

I was drenched in blood bleeding profusely. I could feel the blood gushing out every time my heart would beat.

I had on a white shirt and it was all covered in blood. A guy came and tried to drive me to the hospital and I told him to drive me to my parent's house. I was afraid and wasn't sure I was going to live much longer and wanted to be with my family.

When I got to my parents house, my daughter was in the upstairs window and seen me with all the blood over my shirt. She started screaming to my father, "Papa, my mommy is outside covered in blood."

My father got out of his sick bed and drove me to the hospital. When we arrived at the hospital, they immediately took me to the back. The doctor stapled up my head, and they release me to go home.

Several months later my head was healed up but I was left with a permanent scare from the bottle cuts. The next time I seen the guy that hit me he was paralyzed in a wheel chair, with a voice box.

I felt so sorry for him and had already forgiven him in my heart, because my addiction had me out there wanting that crack, but truth be told there is no rules on the street.

My life was now spiraling downward, but it didn't stop me I was still getting high. I felt like the rehabilitations, or hospitals couldn't help me and I wasn't helping myself.

I began seeing this guy that I liked a lot his name was Tony. We became very close; even though we got high together our relationship was not the typical drug user relationship. He was a good hustler and made big money. We had big fun going to the clubs and shooting pool, which both of us liked to do.

On night we were together and it was getting late in the night hours. Tony wanted me to go home with him, but because I had a business appointment the next day that I had to keep, I didn't go with him and I went home. I knew if I went home with him I wouldn't make that appointment.

The next day I was at my parent's house, and one of his friends came by to let me know that Tony had been shot. When I got to the hospital he was laying in intensive care I found out that the night before while on his way home Tony had got into an altercation with a guy that shot him six times and rode over him with his car, leaving him for dead.

After he was shot he was crawling on the ground for his life, and a man driving a pick-up truck picked him up and threw him in the bed of the truck and drove him to the local hospital and dropped him in front of the emergency entrance. After dropping Tony off in front of the ER, the man in the pick-up truck just drove off.

After surgery all praise to God he survived the gun shots. The doctors were able to remove all the bullets but one. I believe to this day if I had gone home with Tony I would have been shot and would not have been here to tell this story today.

After much rehabilitation Tony got better and decided to move to another state. I wasn't ready to make another move out of the state so I didn't go with him.

Chapter 8

Smith And Wesson

Months later in the late hours of the night I was at my house (the dope house) still no lights, water or gas. It was four of us (two men and two women) in the back room getting high. The two guys got into an argument over money. They began throwing punches and the other girl and I grab the dope and the candle so they wouldn't get knocked over.

The guy that was winning the fight put the other guy out my house. Once he left we continued getting high. I walked in the kitchen carrying my flashlight so I could see where I was going. I saw some illumination from my window. I peeped out the window and one of the cars in my driveway was engulfed in flames. I started screaming for them to come out of the back room. We ran outside to see the flames. Once outside we saw that it was the other female's car that had been set on fire.

My father called the fire department and quickly came across the street; he was so upset with me, because of my lifestyle and my circle of friends.

The next day we couldn't prove it but we felt that the guy that was put out of my house the night before had done it. Not only had he burned up the female's car but he also tried to burn up the guy's van that he had been in the fight with.

We found burned newspaper stuffed down inside the guy's gas tank, looks like he didn't have time to burn both cars even though he did give it a good try.

That morning because I lived on a main street in my city, everyone could see a burnt car in my driveway. It looked like something from a horror movie. Now here I sit in a shell of a house with a total burnt car in my driveway, still getting high.

I would like to believe that this incident would have brought me a moment of clarity, but that didn't even do it for me. As long as I could sit in that back room and get high I was alright.

After a few days the car was hauled away from my driveway and the fire was ruled as arson but no one was charged.

Later in that week I was introduced to a guy that lived on the other side of town that owned his own home. We became friends and I would go over to his house often.

While we're at his home getting high one night; he started acting crazy as he sometimes did. This particular night when he started acting crazy I said, "Ok here we go you about to start acting crazy." He looked at me and slapped me across my face. After he smacked me I said, "You got one more time to hit me." He said, "Or what?" I said you gonna meet smith and wesson." Then he punched me in my face. I reached in my purse and got my gun, and aimed at his leg and pulled the trigger and quickly ran out of his house.

The next day when I woke up and looked in the mirror I had a black eye. After about one week later I called to check on him and he was at home doing fine and he ask me to come over.

When I got there he told me that after I ran out his house he called one of his friends to come take him to the hospital. At the hospital he told them that he shot himself while cleaning his gun.

Now that I think back it's unbelievable that we were back at his house getting high within two weeks of him meeting smith and wesson. How dysfunctional is that? That's what a life of addiction will do.

Chapter 9

Left Behind

Weeks later me and a male friend of mine was sitting at my house with the candles for lights as we're getting high. After all the dope was gone he ask if I wanted to take a ride. Of course I said, yes.

It was already dark and he was driving toward the country. I looked at him and asked, "Where we going? He answered, "I got this" and he kept driving. Eventually he pulled over on a dirt road, at this point I'm trying to keep my cool, but I'm somewhat skeptical about being this far out this late at night. He put the car in park and gets out on his side.

He was acting strange to me and I was not sure what he was up to so I got out of my side of the car. He walked over to my side of the car and ask, "What's up with you?" I quickly said, "Ain't nothing up, what's up with you?" Then he just grabbed my blouse and tore it open. He held me down on top of the car hood and I began kicking and fighting him off me.

To my surprise when he had me pinned down my eyes adjusted to the dark and our eyes met eye ball to eye ball for a couple seconds. I'm not sure what went through his mind when our eyes met. It was like something clicked in his mind and he wasn't able to do to me what he had planned to do.

He jumped up and let me go and walked back around to his side of the car and got in and drove off. He left me standing in no man's land all alone in the dark with a tore blouse. (I always liked that blouse it was so cute.)

Now I have no choice but to walk, it's late at night and no houses in sight. It seemed like I walked for hours, finally I got closer to the city and wouldn't you know it; the only car that comes my way is a police cruiser.

They pull beside me and ask, "Where are you going walking at this hour of the night?" In a angry tone, while holding my blouse closed I said, "I was with a friend and he tore my blouse and left me." They ask me my name, I told them and they ran my name through their system and said they had a warrant for my arrest for old traffic fines. I thought to myself, "This can't be happening."

They hauled me off to jail, and I spent the whole weekend there. Nobody even knew where I was cause I never called home. While in jail I was there with women that I knew from the street. As a matter of fact I knew everyone of them that was in there.

As I looked around I did my own private survey and said to myself, "Every woman in here including myself is in here because of a addiction." I always felt like it was a poor man's rehab, but that's the night I realized it's really a place where people are crying for help.

One female was a heroin addict and she would lay in her bunk crying for help. It seemed like they gave her something for her withdrawals, but it was just not enough for her pain. Truth is I was wishing they would have given me something for my addiction pain too.

As I lay in my bunk, I was thinking the police didn't do me any favors by bringing me to jail. If only I could have made the walk all the way home and continued about my business.

The next morning I went to court and they release me after making me set up a payment plan for the old fines.

Chapter 10

Going Going Gone

Back in the saddle at my house; where the dust has settled from the burnt car being towed out of my driveway. It was now a full bloom drug house, known as the spot. People were running in and out like it was the soul train line.

I had candles and flashlights laying all around the house for the people that would come by. I went and filled up jugs of water from across the street at my parent's house and stacked them up in the corner of my kitchen. I started sleeping in that dark house by myself so I wouldn't miss anyone in case they came by and wanted to smoke their dope.

I still had some of my furniture like my couch, love seat, chair kitchen table, one bed and a dresser. None of it was worth anything because if it was I would have sold that too.

I had already sold the nice pieces of furniture that my grandmother left to me; like the lamps, dressers, bedroom suite, washer, dryer, clothes, dining room set, end tables, shoes, even my grandmother's full length fur coat. I even sold everything in the garage; including a nice barbecue grill, and John Deer riding lawnmower for sixty-dollars, I got three twenty dollar rocks. Everything she left to me was going, going and gone. My only concern was feeding my addiction.

It's Friday night, me and my girl hanging out at the club just having a good time. By this time I already had one too many drinks, and who do I see across the club floor. It was the no good rapist that tried to rape me and left me on the side of the road.

Alcohol never settled well with me, other drugs made me passive but when I drink alcohol it made me act really crazy.

I showed my girlfriend from Youngstown, Ohio who he was and told her what happened. He walked outside and we went out behind him. My girlfriend and I walked behind him as she got up close to him she started calling him curse names.

In a loud and angry tone I said, "Why did you tear my blouse and leave me on the side of the road?" My girlfriend picked up a rock off the ground and threw it at him. He pulled out a razor and swung at my girlfriend, but the razor missed her body.

We began arguing really loud and a guy that I knew for many years walked up and looked at me while asking the rapist, "Hey what's up?" The rapist said, "This ain't none of your business." My male friend said while looking at me, "She is my business." The rapist swung his razor at my male friend and sliced his shirt, but missing his chest. Things got really heated at that point and someone had called the police and they arrested me, my girlfriend, and the rapist that night.

Here I am in the cruiser going back to jail again. While in jail this time I went to church, AA meetings and even played ping pong a lot. I hated being closed off from the rest of the world, and the food was only enough to keep you alive.

On the hearing date me and my girlfriend went in front of the judge and got released. Straight out the jail gate I went right back to getting high. I never told my brother's about what happened to me, because I knew they would have hurt the rapist very bad.

A couple weeks later, I found out that my girlfriend who helped me argue with the rapist left the strip club where she worked and was found dead slumped over the steering wheel of her car with her throat cut. The sad truth is I don't believe that the police ever really put any work into investigating her death.

Sitting in my house with about five people and we're blazing up getting plenty high. There was a knock at my door and I looked out to see who it was, and to my surprise it was my best friend (Carolyn) standing patiently waiting for me to answer.

At that moment, even though I've always loved her I hated for her to see me in the state that I was in. She has always been a true friend to me, she loves God and always stayed true to her relationship with Him. So much so that she would give me the pep talks about getting some help for my life but she never judged me. As grateful as I was for the friendship sometimes I just didn't want to face her because of the embarrassment that I felt.

There were times when she would knock and I would act like I wasn't there by not answering the door. Even though she never said anything I'm sure she knew I was in there.

This time I let her in and she walked in and sat in the living room in my big lazy boy chair. She knew what was going on in the back room even though she never said anything. She looked up at me and said in a calm tone, "Sit here on my knee." I sat down in her lap and she cradled me in her arms and prayed out loud for me. Tears rolled down my face like water from a faucet.

Chapter 11

Pay Up

Late one evening at my house I heard a knock and when I answered the door it was an old friend that I had not seen in several years. I was shocked to see him and when he walked in I said, "Hey Rico, haven't seen you in a minute what's gong on?" He said, "Been thinking about you and came to see if you want to make a change in scenery and come stay with me in Cleveland, Ohio, I'm thinking about stacking my money to go back to Puerto-Rico."

Rico was a good looking Puerto-Rican that I always was attracted to. This sounded like a good plan because I needed to get out of this city for a change of pace

Rico was a high-roller and he didn't use his own product. He was all about making the money, even though he did smoke weed and drink his brown liquor.

He would only allow select people to his home to buy product but no one could come after eleven o'clock and everybody that knew him knew the rule.

Me and Rico did a lot of nice things together, like going out to eat dinner, enjoying ourselves at the clubs and he'd always take me shopping for a nice outfit.

Rico had a very nice and quiet place and I was always comfortable around Rico because he knew my track record of getting high and he was ok with leaving me with something to smoke by myself.

While he was out late this one particular evening making money, I was there alone and three guys came to the door and ask for him. I told them he was sleep, even though I knew he wasn't home.

One of the guys pushed through the door and all three of them rushed in. One of the guys held me, while one of them found a piece of rope and tied my hands behind my back. Then two of them ransacked the house, while the other held me down.

After coming out the bedroom one of the guys said, "I thought you said Rico was here sleep." I said, "He's out." The guy said, "We know he's out but out where, and where's the money?" I said, "I don't know where he is and I don't know anything about no money, because he don't tell me nothing about his business."

They put me in the car with them as a hostage and took me to a house on the other side of town in Cleveland, Ohio. They got me out the car and we all went into this house. They sat me on the couch,

49

and untied my hands. One of them picked up the telephone, told me what to say and then told me to call Rico. Rico answered, and I said, "These three men have me tied up, holding me hostage until you give them the money that you owe them." He said in a serious tone; "Put one of them clowns on the telephone."

The man that seem to be in charge got on the telephone and said, "We don't want to hurt your girl, but you need to give us the money you owe us, you can meet me at the edge-water park, and you better have our five thousand dollars!"

When the man got off the telephone he told the other two guys that Rico wants to meet with him alone. He grabbed me by the arm and took me outside with him. He put me in the back seat of his car and told me to lay down. He got in the driver seat and pulled off. I did exactly what he said, and while laying on the seat my mind was thinking, "Would Rico really pay the money, does he really care enough to give it up, and if he does pay will they still kill me?"

The car finally stopped, the driver got out and left me in the back seat face down. I can hear Rico in a loud tone asking "Where's Melinda?" Then after a few minutes the driver opened the car and told me to get out. I can feel the gun pushing in my back as he said, "Walk slow." I was taking baby steps, toward Rico as he was standing about one hundred feet away from us.

Once we got close enough to Rico, I could see from the expression on Rico's face something wasn't right. He stretched out his arm with the envelope in his hand, and the guy with the gun pushed me over toward Rico and said in a angry tone, "Pay up" as he grabbed the envelope from Rico. The guy walked away while looking inside the envelope.

Rico said to me, "Hurry up let's go now." By then the guy with the gun had realized that the bills were all twenties and fives; that were wrapped around a lot of one dollar bills, to make it look like it was a lot of money.

We ran really fast toward the car and by the time we reached Rico's car the guy turned around and began shooting his gun saying, "This ain't no five-grand!" I jumped into the back seat of Rico's car and he peeled off.

We didn't go back to Rico's house because we knew that would be the first place they would look. Rico drove back to my home town and we went to my house. Rico had a flesh wound in his shoulder from old dude shooting like he was crazy.

Rico began making plans to catch a flight back to Puerto-Rico, and he wanted me to come with him. I contemplated it in hopes for a real change in my life. I came to the conclusion that Rico was a very nice and good looking guy, with a great personality, but he loved that fast money and the thug life. His lifestyle had me being held hostage and I could have lost my life; it was time for me to let him go, so the answer was no. I let him catch the flight alone and I stayed in my hometown.

Several months later I got a blank post card from Mexico, I always thought the post card was from Rico; as a sign letting me know that he's ok.

Chapter 12

The Devil Was Out

It was the holiday season and a few friends and myself were getting high at my house in the backroom as usual. Two of the men started arguing and fighting about the drugs. I ask one of them to leave, after a few minutes he went out the door very angry.

About an hour later we heard glass shattering. I ran into the kitchen and my big picture window was busted and glass was all over my kitchen floor. I couldn't believe it!

It was freezing cold outside with snow all over the ground, the cold air was blowing into my house which was already cold because of no gas, but now it's really freezing cold.

I looked out the busted window and there's the guy that I just put out my house standing by my porch. I opened my door and hit him with one of those hard wooden canes across his head; I hit him so hard that I broke the cane. That slowed him down some, and the police came and took him to jail. By that time everyone had left my house because of all the commotion.

I got a big piece of cardboard and put it up to my big picture window. By the time it got really late the wind was coming through up and around the cardboard into the house. It was like being outside in the ten degree weather, but that didn't stop me from getting high.

The next night I was in my house alone it was extremely cold and about seven inches of snow with ice on the ground. I will never forget it because it was about minus ten degrees outside that night. I said to myself let me get out of this cold house before I freeze to death, because ain't nobody coming out in this cold weather tonight.

Just as I was about to leave and go to my parents house someone was pulling up in my driveway. I said to myself, "If this ain't the devil,." I really thought nobody would be out in this weather but to my surprise the devil was out."

Ray walked in my house as smoke is coming out both of our mouths from the freezing cold. We went to the back room with the candles and flashlights and sat down and got high.

He told me that the guy that busted my window had to get twenty stitches in his head and ear. As we were still getting high I said, "He lucky I didn't shoot him."

When Ray left my house it was sunrise and I began to reflect on how I got to this point. I took a long look at my life and how it had become a mess.

I looked out the window and seen my mother walking over to my house. Normally she doesn't ever come over here because they know what goes on in this house. They choose to pray for me and leave me alone as an adult because of the lifestyle I have chosen to live. So I was very surprised to see her walking over to my house.

She knocked on the door and came in; she sat down at the kitchen table. Wouldn't you know it while my mother was there someone came by to get high, but at that moment, I wanted to hear what my mother was saying so I told the person to come back at another time.

My mother said in calm tone, "Melinda you got to get some help." I said, "I know mom, I will get some help, but the rehabs and those places isn't working for me."

I seen tears rolling down her face, I could tell she was really trying to reach me. I believe I heard her words that day verses any other day.

Chapter 13

Missing Person

After continuing to get high for the next several months I felt like the drug addiction is what I would always be attached to. I went to rehabilitation centers two more times, and each time I relapsed.

Even though I was still getting high for some reason Sunday's became a day that I didn't want to do any drugs. My brother even said to me once, "I notice you don't light up on Sunday's." He was right, but I made up for it during the rest of the week.

I went back to trying to stay clean. I was in AA again; I even had a sponsor this time that I listened to; I was following the program steps and was only hanging around positive people.

After all is said and done I relapsed again, and I learned that each relapse only gets worse and worse, taking me to rock bottom; which is where I had landed.

I decided I needed to get away for a while, I began to think about where to go; a friend that lived in the county came to my mind. He always tried to get me to come and stay with him but I would never go. Now I felt this was the time, so I called him and ask if I could come stay for a while just to rest and have some solitude time. He was glad to hear from me, so I went.

While there he cooked good meals and I got plenty of rest. Because he wasn't into the drug life it made it easier for me to not be concerned about that lifestyle.

During the two weeks out at his home, I never called anyone to let them know where I was, I just wanted that time to myself.

I felt really good and rested after my stay out at my friend's house, so I went to visit my parents. As soon as I walked in the door, my mother looked like she was about to faint. She started crying tears of joy that I was alive.

My brother had heard through street talk that someone had seen me out at a house in the country and I was doing fine. My brother had told my father but because they didn't really know if it was true they still didn't know if I was alright

I never realized that in my absence my mother was really hurting because she thought I could have been dead.

With all the women that were being found dead around the city she was thinking that it could have happened to me because they had not heard from me in weeks. As a matter of fact I later found out that my mother wanted to put a missing person's ad in the newspaper.

The minute I got back into town it was all about people, places, and things, I was back to blazing it up. Then after a while of blazing-up my mindset began to change.

I'm back at my house, but this time I didn't want anybody in the back room or sitting at my table. I was at a point where I wanted to get high alone, I totally isolated myself.

When people would come by most of the time I wouldn't even answer the door, even when I thought they might have something to smoke.

The traffic began to slow down, and I would sit at my house for many days and nights getting high all alone by choice.

It was on a Sunday morning and I walked across the street to my parent's house. As always my mother ask me to come go to church with her. For some reason I did go with her this particular morning.

We arrived at Glenn Christian Church and at prayer time they ask did anyone have any specific request for prayer. I stepped out of the aisle and walked up to the front and said, "My request is to be delivered from drugs." The minister laid hands on me and prayed and just like other times I received the prayer but at that moment I didn't feel any different.

Later in the week I would find myself blazing up from time to time, but this time was not like any other time that I had used drugs. Even though I was still getting high, I felt like deliverance had taken place in my life.

The next week I told my parents that something had happened to me. The craving that I once had for crack cocaine was no longer with me. The next Sunday I went back to church with my mother, Pastor Glenn said, "Does anybody have anything good to say?" A lady raised her hand and said, "I'm healed from diabetes." Everyone clapped and praised God. Then I raised my hand and said, "I'd like to thank God for delivering me from crack cocaine, all the cravings, and all the desires of the drug is gone." Then Pastor Glenn while looking at me asked, "No desire?" I answered, "Yes no desire, or cravings, God has set me free."

After that day my whole life changed. My life has now become a challenge, even though I didn't want the drug life, but I found that the life still wanted me.

A few times different people would come by my house with drugs wanting to sit and chill and blaze up. I looked every one of them right in the eye and said, "I don't get high anymore." I had come to the conclusion with the help of God that I didn't want to be addicted to drugs for the rest of my life.

I made a decision to move in with my parents and my house sat there empty for months and eventually I ended up losing it.

By this time my father had become deathly ill and he passed away. This was a great pain for me that I had to face without the mass of the drug.

My mother moved out their home and into an apartment and I moved in with her. While living with her she truly was a great encouragement to me as well as my best friend.

I was living life on life's terms, I was consistently going to church and my prayer life became very strong as I learned to just talk to God from my heart. I was even asked to speak at different churches to share my testimony giving God all the praise for my deliverance.

Before long I got a job and was able to put some money in my pocket. As time went on I got an apartment of my own.

It was like God had given me back all the years that I had lost with my mother and children. I always like the portion of the scripture that says "And I will restore to you the years that the locust hath eaten," Joel 2:25 KJV.

By now my oldest daughter is done with college and out on her own and has been hired into a lucrative position.

My twins are now teenagers and were living with their grandmother who had become ill. Not long after I moved into my apartment the twin's grandmother passed away and the twins moved in with me.

Chapter 14

Get Busy Living

Me and a male friend were out riding about ten o'clock one night. We began discussing where we would go and eat. Finally we came to the conclusion to go to one of our favorite restaurants.

As we are talking and enjoying the drive to the restaurant, I felt a very hard impact hit the car head on. I could hear the grinding of the metal as it was smashing.

It was so sudden that before I knew it the motor of my friend's car shifted into the front seat. It was only a very small space for us to get out of the car so we both crawled out through the passenger side. Once out of the car we were both sitting on the grass in pain and in shock. Some woman came and put a blanket around me.

The couple that hit us had walked across the street, I could hear the woman hollering from her pain, and the driver was trying to comfort her.

Once the ambulance arrived, I remember trying to touch my legs to make sure I had all my limbs, but there was so much pain in my left wrist. When I got to the hospital, the doctors said my wrist was crushed and they needed a specialist to take a look at it. Once the bone specialist came into the room and assessed me he said I needed to have metal plates put in my wrist and this would require surgery tonight. After the doctors walked out of the room to go and discuss my options; I prayed a sincere prayer asking God not to allow me to have surgery because I didn't want any metal objects in my body.

The doctors returned and said, we have decided that we're not going to do the surgery we're going to cast up your wrist. I was happy but still in pain. They wrapped up my wrist and allowed the wrapping to get hard and then casted over the wrapping. I wore the cast for a little over five months. Wouldn't you know that it had to be the holiday season, during the time that I wore the cast.

With me being a left handed person I realized that all the things we take for granted everyday, like combing my hair and brushing my teeth, tying my shoes or just eating with utensils was a challenge. I couldn't even drive a car, which means I couldn't be mobile around town on my own.

I found myself in a place of depression, and sadness. I was afraid to ride with people in a car because I would have flashbacks of the car accident.

The day came for me to go and get the cast off my wrist and it didn't come fast enough. My wrist was still very weak; as a matter of fact I couldn't even lift a half gallon of milk. I was still feeling depressed as well as angry with the couple for crashing into us.

Now it's time for physical therapy three times a week. While sitting in the waiting room there was an elderly gentleman sitting in the chair next to me and I began telling him what happened with my wrist. He said to me, "If all that you have is a crushed wrist from an accident like that you should be thankful; you could have been paralyzed, in a wheel chair for the rest of your life, or even killed."

At that moment when he said those words to me they penetrated my heart it was like a light bulb came on. Every word he said became clear to me and I knew it was time for me to come out of any type of depression, or anger and get busy living.

About a month later I was at Walgreen's and I saw the guy that crashed into us. I approached him standing at the magazine rack and ask, "Do you know who I am?" He said, "No." I said, "I'm the woman you crashed into on Parkman Rd."

He turned and looked at me with a concerned expression and said, "I'm sorry that happened." He then hung his head down. I said in a calm tone, "I forgive you" and I gave him a hug. During our conversation he told me that neither his girlfriend nor he was badly hurt. I ask him his name and he told me what his name was and I never forgot it.

I freed myself that day; it was like something was lifted off me. To this day we see each other in different spots around the city and we'll stop and hold a conversation.

That mother's day my three girls gave me a heart bracelet, and I wear it to this day on my left wrist as a reminder that I didn't have to be; but I'm still here with my girls.

Chapter 15

Looking For Love

My mother is now in a state of dementia and could not be left alone. I made a decision that she would be better off in the nursing home where she could be seen about twenty-four hours a day. She actually enjoyed all the activities that the nursing home had them participate in. I would go and get her and bring her to my apartment on many occasions for home visits.

She stayed at the nursing home about two years and one night I got a call from the nursing home letting me know that she had been transported to the emergency room of the local hospital.

By the time I got there they told me they couldn't get any vitals and she had passed away.

This was an extremely sad time for me, and I missed her so much. All the advice she use to give me, it was like she always knew what to say at the right moment. My comfort was that I knew she was in heaven and I knew I would see her again.

Now that my mother is gone the girls and I are spending a lot of quality time together, and it was really good.

During this time my love life felt empty, even though I had a male companion that I spent time with periodically.

I did meet a guy that I thought I could just be friends with. We did things like going out of town on different outings, we went to the movies, dinner and it was a lot of fun in the beginning of the relationship.

However the fun didn't last long, he was into things that I knew God didn't want for my life yet, I continued to see him a lot longer than I had ever anticipated.

I tried to break it off a few times but the chemistry between us was very strong, and I would always go back. You could term it as he was my new drug; it was like I was addicted to him. I never realized that you could be addicted to a person, now I know it to be true in my own life.

Eventually my male companion friend and my new male friend both knew about one another, and I wasn't proud of it; in fact I was embarrassed about it. As long as they would stay out of each other's way it was all good with them.

So here I am still spending time with my male companion and my new male friend who has now become an addiction to me. This relationship with my new friend got toxic, especially when he would drink alcohol.

I knew I needed to take a good look at my life and make the right choices being I had daughters that were growing into young women. However, it wasn't a quick process breaking away from the relationship.

Chapter 16

Where There Is Smoke

While my daughter Candi was in Vegas enjoying a short time away from home, myself and my daughter Brandi were fast asleep until about 5:00 o'clock a.m.

Brandi came rushing in my room and she said, "Mommy the apartment building is on fire." I jumped up out my sleep and I smelled smoke. I could even hear the fire crackling. Brandi yelled, "I already called 911!"

As I'm hurrying to get my sweat pants on I looked at my daughter who looked really scared and I'm trying to keep her calm by saying, "Don't worry baby, we are not leaving this earth in a fire."

We hurried toward the apartment door to leave out, and when I turned the door knob and cracked the door open to peep out; I could see the thick smoke swirling in the hallway, and I could hear the loud alarm system going off.

I felt in my spirit not to go out the door, but before I could do anything, I felt a presence of a strong breeze come by me and quickly shut the door.

I said to Brandi, "We're going to wait out on the balcony." While on the balcony, the fire trucks took a long time. It was cold, we were not sure if the building was going to blow, and I wanted me and my daughter off that balcony. My brother 'Mark' also stayed in the complex and was already outside standing down on the ground with a blanket waiting for the fire truck to come and get us down. I decided to take one of my legs and put it over the iron railing, just as I was about to put the other leg over the railing, Brandi, yelled "Mommy here come the firemen running from the parking lot with the hose and the ladder."

Finally after making their way through all the snow that was on the ground, they got to us. The big glass window that set up high in the entrance of the building busted out and a big piece of glass fell on the neck of one of the fireman. If that fireman would not have had on all his gear the big piece of glass that fell on the back of his neck would have taken his head off.

While climbing down the ladder our hands were froze, when we hit the ground, my brother "Mark" covered us with the blanket and we went to his unit to get warmed up.

That morning the fire was in the newspaper with the chief of the fire department giving words regarding the start of the fire. A few of us from the complex went to the Red Cross and explained the situation and our needs for shelter. They took my information and said they would call me. Later that day I got a call from them and they put me and my girls up in the Best Western Motel for a few days.

Later that day we were allowed to go back to the apartment for a few minutes to see if there would be any belongings that were not damaged. While walking up to the third floor a few other people were also in their apartment and told us that they had lost everything in the fire.

We walked up to my apartment door it was burned to a crisp. I push the door open, and I was shocked to see that we had not lost anything. The worst damage that was done was the bottom of my couch had soot on it.

The fire chief walked in and asks me, "Is it normally cold in your apartment?" I answered, "Sir, it's always cold in these apartments, our heat is controlled by the office and when we get cold we are forced to use our ovens to heat up our apartments, because they never turn up the heat high enough for us to get warm."

The fire chief said, "It appears that the fire started from across the hallway due to the stove being used for heat." I immediately thought it was a blessing that nobody got hurt, because the couple across the hallway where the fire started had a small baby to keep warm.

While we were getting some clothes and personal things to take with us we saw the fire chief and his workers moving the stove out of the other apartment from across the hallway for investigation.

A few days later we went back to the apartment to get some more of our personal items and the fire chief was there and he was somewhat angry. He said, "I need you to get all your things moved out of this apartment, it's unsafe, very dangerous, and this place could cave in any day." So we put some smaller things in the car and I knew I would need to get some help with moving all the heavy pieces of furniture.

I got busy looking for a new place to live and the Lord blessed me to find another apartment, and I was very grateful.

At this time there were two men in my life, and the children's father was still in their lives. They all showed up to help me and my children move everything out of the apartment.

While they were there I could tell there was a little tension among them, but I was so focused on getting moved out of the apartment that I said to them, " Ya'll ain't gotta like each other, but please respect one other, now everybody grab a bag so we can get this stuff moved out of this apartment."

Once out of that apartment, we were getting settled into our new apartment. It was time to try and bring a civil case against this apartment complex. I went and spoke to the other people that lived in the unit who were also involved in the fire.

I had the meeting date and time set up for that following Saturday about 2:00 o'clock p.m. When I got to the meeting location, no one showed up accept me and Brandi.

I still pursued the case and hired a lawyer and the lawyer willingly accepted the case. We settled out of court for an undisclosed amount of money.

There is a scripture that means so much to me Isaiah 43:2 (KJV) "When thou walkest through the fire, thou shall not be burned."

Coming Through The Storm

Letting Go

By this time I'm no longer addicted to drugs but I'm addicted to this toxic man. He was the type of man that when he drank he got abusive. Everyone around me that cared anything about me would tell me that he was not good for me but I wasn't trying to hear what they were saying. It was like I had to have him.

We continued to date for a while, the first time he hit me I was in shock. He smacked me in my face so hard that I had a black eye, and of course I tried to hide it so know one would know he was being physically abusive.

This went on for a while from time to time and he would always buy me some roses and apologize by saying he's sorry. Then things would go back to normal with everything being back cool again.

We went out of the state to visit some friends, and we got into a huge argument while we were there. He threw me down on the floor and we were tussling; I was trying to get up, but he began choking me and I screamed, "Take your hand off of me in the name of Jesus." He had a look in his eyes that I'd never seen before. He took his hands off of me and I got up and ran to my car and drove back to Ohio by myself.

That was the last time he put his hands on me because I knew I deserved to be treated better than that. I made a choice to have nothing else to do with him after that night.

Chapter 17

Not In Your Back Yard

After going through so much drama in my life, my three girls came to me and ask if I would like to go and celebrate momma Karen's (which is Tanji's mother-in-law) birthday in Jamaica. I was excited and said, "Right on."

I thought about how I really needed a vacation, and Jamaica was one of the places I always wanted to visit. I imagined seeing the clear water; I felt so much joy thinking about being with my children and celebrating momma Karen's birthday.

Me and the twins went to the post office and got passport pictures taken. While waiting for the passports to be finalized, me and the girls went shopping for the trip.

I bought some new luggage; the girls bought cute swim suits. Later I decided I needed a new swim suit too and we went back and picked up a cute one for me.

After a few weeks the passports came in and we went and picked them up. A few days later we were all off to the airport. So me, momma Karen, her husband Wool, Candi, Brandi, Tanji and her husband Eric all mobbed up at the airport check-in.

In one plane; myself, Tanji, Eric, Candi, and Brandi rode together and in the other plane momma Karen and Wool rode together, and their plane took off about an hour before ours.

After the long plane ride we arrived in Jamaica. Once off the plane and on the resort the breath taking beauty hit me right in the face. Many people say that there is so much poverty there, but take it from me there's parts of Jamaica that is so beautiful it's truly breath taking.

As we're getting checked-in at the resort, we notice that momma Karen and Wool's plane has not arrived. Tanji checked with the desk clerk to see if the other plane that her mother and father-in-law was on, had arrived yet.

After some research on where the other plane was we found out that momma Karen and Wool's plane was traveling for a couple hours and had to make an emergency landing somewhere near Atlanta.

The plane was leaking break fluid and had a malfunction with stopping. Once the plane was able to do an emergency landing they had all the passengers transfer to a new plane to continue the flight into Jamaica.

It seemed like forever waiting for momma Karen and Wool's plane to come in. Finally they arrived safe and sound.

We were glad to see them and momma Karen seemed at peace. She said that when the malfunction happened on their plane she immediately went to praying. I wasn't surprised that she was praying being the woman of God that she is.

Everyone decided to put the incident behind us and have a good time on this vacation for momma Karen's birthday.

While in my room at the resort, I stood on the balcony. I could see the Caribbean Sea and it looked amazing. I could see and hear the big waves as they were crashing against the rocks and it felt like God was saying to me, "Welcome, I am God and I'm here with you."

The next day we had a birthday celebration for momma Karen. We played games, danced, after a while we cut the cake and had some ice cream and enjoyed one another's company.

The third day in Jamaica I wrote a few things down on paper that I wanted to let go out of my life. I said to the twins, "Let's go get in the water, and I don't want to get into no swimming pool I want to go straight into the Caribbean Sea."

I wanted to be able to say that I swam in the Caribbean Sea. They agreed to go to the sea with me and I folded up the piece of paper and put it down in my bathing suit top.

We went to the water and got in; when I looked up toward the sky the sun was shinning very bright and reflecting off the water. Me and the twins were having a great time splashing water in the Caribbean Sea.

I pulled out my piece of paper and I waited for a big wave to come my way and I let the wave take the paper into the Caribbean Sea and I said it was symbolic of letting go of all the negative stuff in my life.

I began to think about how Carolyn once said she was going to have a bomb fire and we would write all the negative things in our lives down on an index card and we would throw them into the fire as a sign of letting go. We never got around to it because things kept coming up. Now I have taken this opportunity to do it right here in Jamaica.

When I let that piece of paper go into the waves, I felt a release and a silent peace inside of me, and then tears began to roll down my face.

Day four I walked to the hut bar outside the resort. I ordered a Jamaica punch and went and took a seat at one of the tables. A male server came walking toward me with my drink on top of his head. I was wondering how he kept that drink on his head without it falling. So I asked him, and he said he had been doing it for a long time and had become very good at it.

He handed me my drink and said, "Here's the drink for a pretty lady." We struck up a conversation and he told me his name was Marley, I said "Wow like Bob Marley?" He said yes but Marley is my first name. He asked me my name and where I was from. I told him my name and that I was from Ohio; he told me that he has relatives back in New York. He also told me that he also worked in the Ganja fields. I later found out that it was a marijuana field.

Later that day; me, Tanji, Eric, Candi, and Brandi had a guide and went off the resort. We went to the hood and we bought T-shirts that were only $5 which were much cheaper than the resort price, we also bought other souvenirs that were priced reasonable.

After we finished shopping the tour guide took us to his home which was in a better part of Jamaica. He lived with his mother and she made us a full course dinner. His mother went in the back yard and made some cherry juice from the cherries off their tree.

After we ate a nice dinner, the guide took us to a tourist location called Rick's Cafe Cliff. While we were there Candi being in college and majoring in telecommunications had her camera equipment with her and asked one of the natives if she could interview him on film for a piece that she was doing called; "You Won't See This In Your Backyard." He agreed and sat down and answered her interview questions.

Then we walked over to the cliff as she continued to film him and just before he jumped off the high cliff into the water he yelled, "You won't see this in your back yard!" He jumped off the cliff doing triple somersaults before his dive into the water. It was like something we had never seen before in our lives, he was really amazing. Candi filmed the entire jump and when he came back up out the water we all gave applaud by clapping.

We ended the day by going to the Dunn's River Fall in Ocho Rios Jamaica. We did some rock climbing starting from the bottom to the top. Afterwards we went to a sport's bar and shot some pool, danced, and had a good time.

I began to feel a little tired and went back to our room at the resort and laid across the bed. I dozed off for a little while and when I had awakened it was after 1:00 o'clock in the morning.

I called Candi and Brandi's cell phones but neither of them answered. I called Tanji's cell phone and asked her where was the twins? She answered, "Ah mommy don't start they alright, go to bed." I tried to go back to sleep but I couldn't. I called the front desk and ask if anyone had seen my daughters, the man that answered the telephone ask me, to give him a description. He took all the information and said he would call me back, because there's nothing open at this hour at the resort.

After about ten or fifteen minutes he called me back and said he had not found any girls matching that description and said he has decided to close down the hotel resort not allowing anyone in or out until the girls are located.

I thought to myself, I done had them shut down this resort and I'm not feeling guilty because I need to know where my children are; because nothing is open at this hour and we're in another country.

About twenty minutes later he called back and said we have located them both and they are headed back to the room. I asked him, "Where were they?" He said, "They were in the kitchen area with a couple of the workers talking and laughing."

When Candi, and Brandi got to the room they were light weight salty and embarrassed that I had the resort shut down looking for them. I told them if they would have just answered their cell phone we would have avoided all this. I guess they thought about it and agreed with me because we all went to sleep peacefully.

Day five before we left we went to a few live shows that was really entertaining. On our way out while boarding the plane to head back to Ohio, I was looking out the window watching the plane as its nose was going in an upward position; looking down toward the resort thinking how beautiful Jamaica was and how much fun I had; a tear rolled down my cheek.

Chapter 18

Game Changer

Two years later as I'm continuing to walk in my sobriety we found out Tanji was pregnant. This was the most exciting news because this would be my first grandchild. It would also be the first grandchild on Tanji's husband's side of the family.

In my heart I knew I would be better at being a grandparent because of all the mistakes that I made in the past with my three girls. God was giving me back some of the years that I had regretfully missed with my children.

Once Tanji arrived at the hospital and settled into the delivery room, the waiting room was filled with my side of the family and Eric's side of the family. I mean the room was really crowded and everyone was filled with anticipation, while waiting for the doctor to come out.

Once the doctor came in and said it was a baby boy we all began cheering and clapping. Everyone was so excited to have a new arrival to the family.

When I made it to the back to take my first look at my grandson and held him in my arms there is no other feeling that I can describe that compares to holding my first grandchild.

We had two names that we were trying to decide between and I didn't like either of them, so for days before Tanji was released we were all trying to decide what was my first grandson's name going to be.

Finally Brandi came up with the name "Trenton" and we all agreed. As a matter of fact I loved it!

I was so grateful to God for allowing me this moment to share with my new grandson and my family. At this moment nothing else mattered to me because I was so overwhelmed with my new grandson. I knew in my heart Trenton would be a game changer for our entire family.

Freeing Myself

At this point I had to do some soul searching because in my past I had lost a lot of people in my life that was very close to me. When my mother died I knew she was with the Lord but I was still sad and mad. I felt as though she still had more years in her. I would sit by myself on the edge of my bed and just cry thinking and praying about the people that I had lost. Including my brother Mark and then a year later my brother Dave died right behind him. After that it was my aunt Jackie who was my mother's sister died shortly after Dave. I decided I needed to get some counseling to talk with someone, because it was so many deaths right behind one another.

I realized that I had been holding on to all this anger inside of me because so many people that I loved so much had left me.

The counseling was helpful and I finally decided to give it all to God. I prayed from the depths of my heart and I asked God to help me to forgive and let go of this anger that I was holding inside of me for all the people that had left me, Mommy, Mark, Dave Aunt Jackie, and also all the bad relationships that I had dealt with.

After that prayer I felt healed, like something heavy had been lifted off of me. I felt like I was running and shedding all the hurt and pain. Today I'm here to tell you I'm free, and I mean from drugs, alcohol, sexual sin, men, guilt, loneliness, unhealthy relationship & and friendship. I have forgiven all of them the way that I forgave the guy years earlier that had drove into us head on in the car crash.

I was once told by a friend whose name is (Marvin) he said, "Don't be like Lot's wife in the Bible; but never look back."

Yes I have my days, but I always pray and look to God whenever something comes my way and I'm going through I just remind God, you are the same God that healed me from cancer, delivered me from drugs, brought me out of a car accident and fire. You have kept me through it all, and I yell up to God these words; "God your word says that You are the same yesterday today and forever." (KJV Hebrew 13:8)

Today I know that all the things I did was never who I was, but it was what I did to fulfill the addiction of drugs that was apart of my life. I thank God for returning me to who I really am.

Coming Through The Storm

Personal Words To My Reader

If I would tell you anything about getting into a good place in your life from any type of addiction it would be this:

Get away form negative people places and things. Find yourself around positive people; never give up even if you mess up. Find you some strong supportive people that will lift you up and not judge you about your mistakes and falls in this life. Remember God is the only true judge.

If God be for us then who can be against us? (KJV Romans 8:31)

Foremost learn to love yourself no matter what state you're in, because God loved me in my mess and then when I called on Him from a sincere heart He showed me who I really was.

I'm here today to tell you if I can do it with the help of God anybody can because there's nothing impossible for Him to do.

I know the plans that I have for you declares the Lord, plans to prosper you and not to harm you. (Jeremiah 29:11)